P9-BBN-701

# The salesclerk made me buy it.

## by Cathy Guisewite

Selected Cartoons from
**A MOUTHFUL OF BREATH MINTS
AND NO ONE TO KISS**
Volume 2

FAWCETT CREST • NEW YORK

A Fawcett Crest Book
Published by Ballantine Books
Copyright © 1983 by Universal Press Syndicate, Inc.

All rights reserved under International and Pan-American Copyright
Conventions. No part of this book may be used or reproduced in
any manner whatsoever without written permission except in the
case of reprints in the context of reviews. Published in the United
States by Ballantine Books, a division of Random House, Inc., New
York, and simultaneously in Canada by Random House of Canada
Limited, Toronto.

Library of Congress Catalog Card Number: 83-71766

ISBN 0-449-20926-1

This book comprises a portion of A MOUTHFUL OF BREATH
MINTS AND NO ONE TO KISS and is reprinted by arrangement
with Andrews and McMeel, Inc., A Universal Press Syndicate
Company.

Manufactured in the United States of America

First Ballantine Books Edition: April 1986
Second Printing: November 1987

WHAT MAKES YOU SUCH AN EXPERT ON DATING SOMEONE AT THE OFFICE, MOM?

I SAW IT ON THE PHIL DONAHUE SHOW.

PHIL POINTED OUT THAT OFFICE DATING PUTS A HIDEOUS STRAIN ON BOTH YOUR WORK AND RELATIONSHIP, AND THE AUDIENCE CHEERED!

THEN PHIL SAID, "BUT COULDN'T A LOVING, DISCREET COUPLE MAKE IT WORK?", AND THE AUDIENCE CHEERED THAT... THEN PHIL GOT EXASPERATED BECAUSE THE SAME PEOPLE KEPT CHEERING FOR OPPOSITE THINGS, AND THE AUDIENCE CHEERED THAT! THEN...

WHAT'S YOUR POINT, MOM?

I FORGOT.

Guisewite

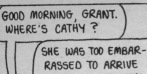

WHAT ARE YOU DOING WHILE GRANT'S OUT OF TOWN?

I'M STARVING MYSELF ON A HIDEOUS DIET...

...TORTURING MYSELF WITH EXERCISES... AND ATTACKING MY FACE, HAIR, AND NAILS WITH BEAUTY TREATMENTS SO I'LL BE GORGEOUS WHEN HE GETS BACK.

CATHY, THIS IS PATHETIC. IF YOU HAD LEFT TOWN, GRANT WOULD BE USING THIS WEEK TO GO OUT WITH EVERYONE IN THE CITY.

THAT'S WHAT MAKES WOMEN SO SPECIAL, ANDREA.

...WE'RE CAPABLE OF ENTERTAINING OURSELVES.

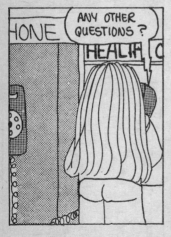

CATHY, HOW DID YOU LOSE 10 POUNDS IN 4 DAYS ??

NEW FAT IS EASIER TO LOSE THAN OLD FAT, ANDREA.

IT'S ALL TIMING. IF YOU GAIN 5 POUNDS IN ONE NIGHT, YOU COULD LOSE IT IN 2 DAYS. BUT IF YOU WAIT A WEEK, FORGET IT.

AFTER A WEEK, THE NEW FAT HAS ALREADY BECOME PART OF YOUR BODY'S FAT FAMILY AND IT'S...

...SOMETIMES I HATE THE THINGS I'M AN EXPERT ON.

Guisewite

NOW THEN... YOU SAID, "THE HEALTH CLUB IS A CENTER FOR INTELLIGENT, SUCCESSFUL, GORGEOUS, MUSCLE-Y MEN."

CORRECT.

BY THAT DID YOU MEAN INTELLIGENT MEN, SUCCESSFUL MEN, GORGEOUS MEN, AND MUSCLE-Y MEN? FOUR DIFFERENT TYPES OF MEN?

OR DID YOU MEAN THE CLUB IS A CENTER FOR MEN WHO HAVE ALL FOUR OF THESE QUALITIES IN ONE?? OR DID YOU MEAN THAT SOME OF THE MEN HAVE SOME OF THESE QUALITIES??

I NEVER SIGN A CONTRACT UNTIL I UNDERSTAND ALL THE FACTS.

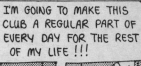

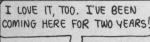

HI THERE, SWEETIE. IT'S ME. I WAS JUST THINKING ABOUT YOU AND, UH, I THOUGHT I'D SAY HELLO.

SO, UM... HA, HA... **HELLO!** OH, HEE, HEE, HEE... AHEM.. THIS IS STUPID.

NO, REALLY, I WAS JUST SITTING HERE AND HEE HEE **HA, HA! HOO HA!** WAIT... I'M.. AHEM..**HOO HA HA HA!!**

EXCUSE ME, MOM. I HAVE TO GO BREAK INTO IRVING'S APARTMENT AND RIP THE TAPE OUT OF HIS PHONE ANSWERING MACHINE.

IF I BUY A PIE AT THE 7-11 AT MIDNIGHT ON JANUARY 5th, EVERYONE WILL KNOW I'M CHEATING ON MY NEW YEAR'S DIET.

SO WHAT? WHAT DO I CARE IF THE CASHIER AT THE 7-11 THINKS I'M CHEATING ON MY DIET?? HAH!

HELLO I WOULD LIKE TO BUY THIS PIE AND I DON'T CARE WHAT YOU THINK!!!

WHAT'S HAPPENED TO YOUR DIET, CATHY?

MY STRONG SIDE KEEPS SHOWING UP AT THE WRONG TIME.

YVONNE BROUGHT THE HOME-MADE SPINACH PASTA, SEASONED WITH HERBS FROM HER WINDOWSILL HERB GARDEN.

RAYMOND HAND-GROUND THE FLOUR FOR HIS LOVELY ALMOND-FIG LOAF, SERVED WITH KIM'S INCOMPARABLE PLUM PRESERVES!

THE KLEINS BROUGHT THE SPECTACULAR BLANCHED CRUDITÉ PLATTER, HOME-GROWN SPROUTS, WITH A DIP OF HOMEMADE YOGURT AND HONEY GATHERED FROM THEIR OWN HIVE!

CATHY IS THE ONE WHO JUST LEFT WITH THE MARSHMALLOW JELLO MOLD IN HER PURSE.

Guisewite

MY OLD BUDDY, ZACK, SPLIT UP WITH HIS WIFE AND ASKED IF HE COULD HANG OUT HERE.

THAT'LL BE NICE FOR YOU, IRVING.

NICE?! I'VE WAITED FOUR YEARS FOR THIS! MY DRINKING BUDDY'S BACK! MY CAROUSING BUDDY! ZACK!!

YEOOWCH!!

IS IT MY IMAGINATION, OR DID SOMEONE JUST BITE ME IN THE KNEE?

IT USED TO BE ALL A GUY NEEDED TO ATTRACT THE LADIES WAS A SPORTS CAR. I COULD HANDLE THAT.

THEN PLANTS. A GUY WITH A FICUS BENJIMINA AND A $2,000 STEREO SYSTEM HAD IT MADE.

...BUT NOW I DON'T SEEM "WITH IT" UNLESS I HAVE A 2-YEAR-OLD AND A BRIEFCASE FULL OF TOYS. CATHY, HOW AM I SUPPOSED TO DO THAT ??!

OH, IRVING...

PATHOS. THE UNIVERSAL CHARMER.

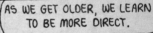

HOW WAS THE BIG DATE LAST NIGHT, CATHY?

MOM, I'M A GROWN, INDEPENDENT WOMAN.

I HARDLY THINK I NEED TO GIVE YOU A REPORT ON EVERY DATE.

CATHY, IF YOU'RE SO INDE-PENDENT, WHY DID YOUR MOTHER EVEN KNOW YOU HAD A DATE LAST NIGHT??

IT SLIPPED OUT WHEN SHE WAS BEGGING ME TO IRON AND HEM HER DRESS.

SHAMPOO I TRIED ONCE AND HATED... COLOGNE I'VE GOTTEN SICK OF... FACE CREAM THAT DIDN'T WORK...

MAKEUP THAT'S THE WRONG COLOR... HAIR CLIPS THAT WON'T STAY IN MY HAIR... BUBBLE BATH THAT I'M ALLERGIC TO...

MY BATHROOM CUPBOARDS ARE FILLED WITH THINGS I WILL NEVER USE, FORCING ME TO THROW THE THINGS I DO USE ALL OVER THE COUNTER!

THE FAMILY TRADITION LIVES ON!!

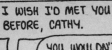

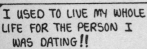